Hands-On Projects

POST OFFICE

Active Learning about Community Workers

by Carol Wawrychuk & Cherie McSweeney
illustrated by Philip Chalk

Contents

Entire contents copyright ©1998 by Monday Morning Books, Inc.
For a complete catalog, please write to the address below:
P.O. Box 1680
Palo Alto, CA 94302 U.S.A.

Call us at: 1-800-255-6049
E-mail us at: MMBooks@aol.com
Visit our Web site:
http://www.mondaymorningbooks.com

Monday Morning is a registered trademark of
Monday Morning Books, Inc.

ISBN 1-57612-038-4
Printed in the United States of America
987654321

Introduction

Mailing a letter — what a mystery that can be to a child! Youngsters wonder, "How does the mail get out of the mailbox?" "Where does the mail come from?" "How does the mail carrier know which house it goes to?" The *Post Office* theme unit answers these and other questions posed by the early learner.

The adventure begins when children recreate the world of the mail carrier. Children delight in creating a post office counter, a large mailbox, and a mail truck. While some youngsters work the register and scale at the post office counter, others deliver letters and packages in the mail truck. Mail carriers wear butcher paper caps and carry letter pouches designed from cereal boxes.

Boys and girls learn about the community as they make a large scale scene complete with a post office and houses. Number and letter recognition is emphasized as children sort envelopes, play an alphabet bean bag toss game, or stamp letters and numbers on packages.

Children's participation in this creative learning environment enriches their skills and their imaginations.

Personal Observations:

The post office doors swung open to reveal children enthralled to be working in the Post Office. Some busily weighed packages and stamped envelopes. Others carefully sorted the mail. Both boys and girls readied the mail truck for deliveries. The first stop was to deliver the daily mail. The last stop was at the corner mailbox where the mail carrier quickly gathered the mail. The letters and packages were swiftly returned to the post office to be processed.

Youngsters concentrated as they transformed juice containers into miniature postal workers to be used in a dramatic play scenario.

The children were challenged by an assortment of activities which focused on letter and number recognition.

The *Post Office* theme unit created spontaneous teamwork. It was thrilling to watch children learn about these important members of their community.

Mail Truck

Materials:

Mail Stencil (p. 6), dryer box (or similar-sized box), flat sections of cardboard, construction paper (red and blue), four thread spools, yarn, tempera paint (black and white), paint rollers, shallow tins (for paint), glue, scissors, sharp instrument for cutting (for adult use only)

Directions:

1. Cut blue and red construction paper into strips.
2. Use the mail stencil to cut out letters. Make a mail sign for each side of the truck.
3. Remove one end of the box.
4. Cut a front windshield and two side windows in the box.
5. To make a gas tank, cut three sides of a square in the rear of the box, and fold back the flap.
6. Cut four tires and a steering wheel from the flat section of cardboard.

Mail Truck

7. Punch two holes in the center of the steering wheel, and punch two holes beneath the windshield.

8. Attach the steering wheel by aligning the holes on the steering wheel with the holes beneath the windshield and tying together with yarn.

9. Punch two holes in the center of each wheel, and punch two holes for each tire on the sides of the box.

10. Thread yarn through the two holes in each tire, bring the two ends of yarn through the opening in a spool, thread the yarn through the two holes in the box, and tie.

 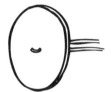 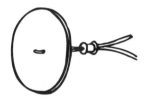

11. Have children paint the mail truck and tires.

12. Once the paint has dried, children can glue the construction paper stripes and Mail sign to the truck.

Option:
• Provide junk mail and packages for children to use with the mail truck.

Book Link:
• *Eye Openers: Trucks* by Ted Taylor (Macmillan)

This pump is from an activity in the book *Firefighters* (MM 2043).

Post Office ©1998 Monday Morning Books, Inc.

Mailbox

Materials:

Box (the size of a two-drawer file cabinet), four square facial tissue boxes, computer paper box lid, large sheet of white construction paper, envelopes, writing paper, pencils, markers, tempera paint (red and blue), shallow tins (for paint), paint rollers, masking tape, glue, sharp instrument for cutting (for adult use only)

Post Office ©1998 Monday Morning Books, Inc.

Mailbox

Directions:

1. Tape the box closed.
2. Cut an opening with a handle and a slot large enough to accommodate the computer paper box lid, according to the diagram below.

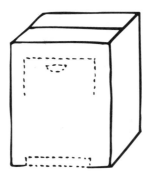

3. Glue the four small square boxes to the bottom of the larger box for legs.
4. Once the glue has dried, the children can paint the mailbox. Provide red paint for the legs of the box and the drawer (box lid) and blue paint for the box itself.
5. Write the word "mailbox" on the white construction paper.
6. Glue the sign to the front of the mailbox.
7. Once the mailbox has dried, provide envelopes, paper, and pencils for children to use to write and mail letters.

Option:
• Save promotional stamps for use in this activity.

Book Link:
• *The Jolly Postman or Other People's Letters* by Janet & Allan Ahlberg (Little, Brown)

Post Office Counter

Materials:

Box (the size of a floor lamp), butcher paper, four cardboard wrapping paper tubes, masking tape, tempera paint (red and blue), paintbrushes and rollers, sharp instrument for cutting (for adult use only)

Directions:

1. Tape the box closed.
2. At each end of the top and bottom of the box, cut holes just large enough for a wrapping paper tube to fit through. (Make sure the holes on the top and bottom are aligned.)
3. Insert one wrapping paper tube into another, and reinforce the joining tubes by wrapping with masking tape. Do this with the remaining tubes.

Post Office Counter

4. Put the tubes in the holes in the box, bringing them slightly through the bottom sets of holes.

5. Cut two slits in the end of each tube, and spread the flaps on the tubes open.

6. Tape the open flaps to the bottom of the box to stabilize the tubes.

7. Cut a piece of butcher paper slightly longer than the box. If the butcher paper is too wide, cut it in half.

8. Have the children paint the box blue and the poles red.

9. Paint "Post Office" in red on the butcher paper.

10. Once the paint has dried, wrap the ends of the sign around the top of the wrapping paper tubes, and secure with masking tape.

Options:

• Write the sign with markers or crayons.

• Provide star stickers for the children to use to decorate the post office sign.

Book Link:

• *The Post Office Book: Mail and How it Moves* by Gail Gibbons (Harper and Row)

Mail Sorting Shelves

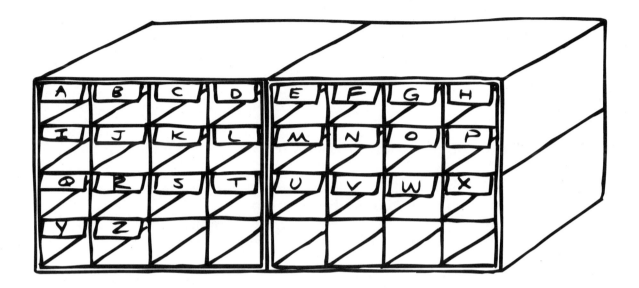

Materials:
Two beverage boxes with cardboard dividers, self-adhesive Velcro strips, tempera paint, sponge pieces, shallow tins (for paint), index cards, markers, transparent tape

Directions:
1. Let children sponge paint the boxes.
2. Once the paint has dried, attach Velcro strips to the sides of the boxes.
3. Attach the two boxes together.
4. Have the children fold the index cards in half and write a letter of the alphabet on the bottom half of each card.
5. Tape the top fold of each card inside one slot of the box.
6. Children can now sort mail according to the alphabet.

Option:
• Glue the boxes together if Velcro is not available.

Puzzle Link:
• *Alphabet Sorting Kit* (Lakeshore)

Post Office ©1998 Monday Morning Books, Inc.

Weight Scale

Materials:
Shoe box, four lightweight springs, construction paper scraps, gift boxes, butcher paper, scissors, markers, transparent tape, masking tape, glue

Directions:
1. Provide construction paper for the children to rip, tear, and glue onto the shoe box and lid.
2. Once the glue has dried, tape the springs to the inside corners of the shoe box and to the bottom of the shoe box lid.
3. Children can use gift boxes, butcher paper, scissors, markers, and transparent tape to wrap packages.
4. Children can weigh the packages on the scale.

Mail Carrier Cap

Materials:

Butcher paper, scrap paper, tempera paint (in assorted colors), paintbrushes, shallow tins (for paint), masking tape

Directions:

1. Cut butcher paper into an 18 in x 18 in (46 cm x 46 cm) square. (Make one per child.)
2. Have children paint scraps of paper, then place the wet scraps over the butcher paper, pat, and remove. They should do this step several times.
3. Once the paint has dried, place each child's butcher paper on top of his or her head to form a cap.
4. Make a band around each cap with masking tape.
5. Remove the formed caps and trim the excess butcher paper, leaving a brim in the front.

Post Office ©1998 Monday Morning Books, Inc.

Mail Carrier Bag

Materials:
Cereal box, butcher paper, crayons or markers, hole punch, yarn

Directions:
1. Remove the inside bag and the top flaps from the cereal box.
2. Cover the cereal box with butcher paper.
3. Punch two holes at the top of one side of the box.
4. Insert yarn through the holes and tie the two ends together in a knot.
5. Provide crayons and markers for children to use to decorate the box.
6. The completed mail carrier bag can be worn over the shoulder.

Options:
• Provide other art materials for children to use to decorate the mail carrier bag.
• Make one bag for children to share, or several bags. Or let each child bring in a cereal box to make into a mail carrier bag.
• Children can stamp envelopes with alphabet and number rubber stamps.
• Children can bring in "junk mail" from home.

Book Link:
• *123 Count with Me* by Sian Tucker (Simon and Schuster)

Puzzle Link:
• *Multi-Ethnic Career Puzzle Set - Mail Carrier* (Lakeshore)

Name Necklace

Materials:
Construction paper, straws, yarn, yarn needle, hole punch, marker, scissors

Directions for One Necklace:
1. Cut straws into small sections.
2. Cut one circle for each letter of a child's name.
3. Write one letter of the child's name on each circle, and punch two holes in the top of the circle.
4. Tie the yarn needle to a long section of yarn, and tie a section of straw to the other end.
5. Have the child string the straws and letters to create his or her name.
6. Once the stringing is completed, remove the needle and tie the loose pieces of yarn together.

Option:
• Large beads or macaroni can be used in place of straws.

Book Link:
• *The Letters Are Last* by Lisa Campbell Ernst (Viking)

 Post Office ©1998 Monday Morning Books, Inc.

City and Country Reversible Backdrop

This activity should be used with the Box Post Office (p. 18), Milk Carton Houses (p. 19), Tissue Box Mail Truck (p. 20), and Mail Carrier (p. 21).

Materials:
Box (the size of a two-drawer file cabinet), tempera paint, paint-brushes or roller, shallow tins (for paint), markers, heavy string or yarn, glue, sharp instrument for cutting (for adult use only), decorative items (tissue paper, self-sticking dots, colored construction paper, dry cereal, macaroni, dried beans, sand paper, pipe cleaners, and Popsicle sticks)

Directions:
1. Cut off the two ends and one side panel of the box.
2. Punch one hole at the top of each of the side panels.
3. Lay the backdrop flat and draw a city scene on one side and a country scene on the other.

City and Country Reversible Backdrop

4. Have children use tissue paper, self-sticking dots, colored construction paper, and markers to decorate the first side.

5. Once the first side has dried, turn the backdrop over and let children use three-dimensional items to decorate it, such as dry cereal, macaroni, dried beans, sand paper, pipe cleaners, and Popsicle sticks.

6. When both sides of the scenes have dried, reinforce the two side panels by tying heavy string or yarn through the two holes.

Note:

Three-dimensional items should only be used on the second side of the backdrop to prevent chipping, breaking, or crushing.

Book Links:

• *Paddington's ABC* by Michael Bond (Puffin)
• *The Story of Zachary Zween* by Makel Watts (Parents' Magazine Press)

Box Post Office

Materials:

Large computer paper box,
tempera paint, paintbrushes,
sponges or rollers, shallow tins (for paint),
markers, sharp instrument for cutting (for adult use only)

Directions:

1. Remove the lid and turn the box upside down.
2. Cut a door and windows in the box.
3. Have the children paint the post office.
4. Once the paint has dried, let children write Post Office on the box. They can add any other details, as well.

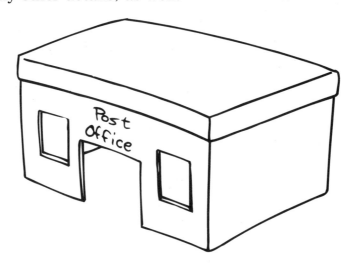

Milk Carton Houses

Materials:

Cardboard milk cartons (in assorted sizes), colored construction paper, tempera paint (in assorted colors), sponge pieces, shallow tins (for paint), glue, scissors, stapler, sharp instrument for cutting (for adult use only)

Directions:

1. Rinse out the milk cartons, and staple the tops closed.
2. Remove the bottom section of each milk carton.
3. Cut a small opening on one side of each carton.
4. Add glue to assorted colors of tempera paint and mix.
5. Have children cut windows and doors from construction paper.
6. Provide the paint and glue mixture for the children to use to paint the houses. They can attach the windows and doors while the paint is still wet.
7. Once the paint has dried, provide construction paper scraps for the children to use to put "mail" into the openings in the houses.

Book Link:

• *A House Is a House for Me* by Mary Ann Hoberman (Penguin)

Tissue Box Mail Truck

Materials:
Rectangular facial tissue box, construction paper (white and black), markers, glue, scissors

Directions:
1. Remove two-thirds of the top of the facial tissue box.
2. Cut a windshield in the front of the box and a window on each side.
3. Cut four wheels from the black construction paper.
4. Have the children tear the construction paper into small pieces and glue the pieces to the tissue box.
5. Have children glue on the wheels.
6. Once the box is dry, provide markers for the children to use to add desired details.

Option:
• Make one truck for children to share, or several trucks. Or let each child bring in a tissue box to make into a mail truck.

Book Link:
• *Truck Song* by Diane Siebert (Harper & Row)

Mail Carrier

Materials:
Clothing Patterns (p. 22), individual-size plastic juice containers without lids (one per child), Styrofoam balls (one per child), construction paper (black, blue, and white), markers, glue sticks

Directions:
1. Rinse out the juice containers.
2. Trace the clothing patterns onto construction paper and cut out. (Make one set for each child.)
3. Children can use markers to draw facial features and hair on the Styrofoam balls.
4. Help each child attach the two parts of his or her mail carrier by pushing the head on the opening of the juice container.
5. Children can attach the clothing to the mail carriers with glue sticks.

Option:
• Small sections of yarn can be glued to the Styrofoam balls for hair.

Book Link:
• *The Jolly Christmas Postman* by Janet and Allan Ahlberg (Little, Brown)

Post Office ©1998 Monday Morning Books, Inc.

Clothing Patterns

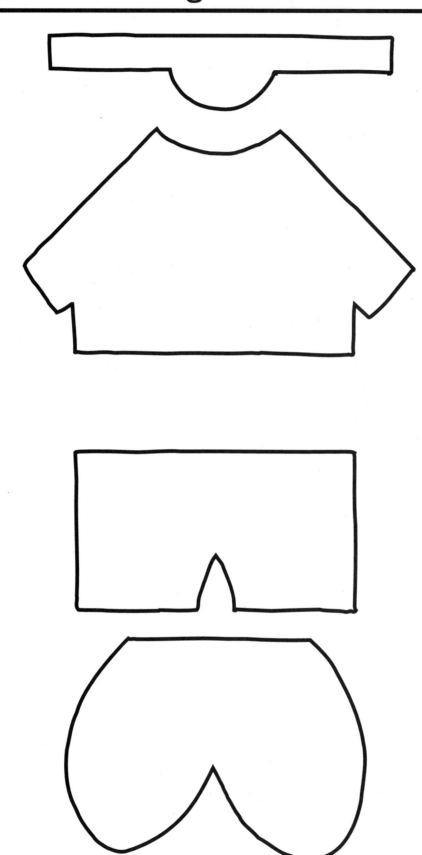

Mail Carrier House

This activity should be used with the Flower Box (p. 26), Paper Flowers (p. 27), and House Mailbox (p. 29).

Materials:

Two large appliance boxes, square facial tissue box, construction paper, white tissue paper, heavy string or yarn, tempera paint, paintbrushes or rollers, shallow tins (for paint), glue, scissors, sharp instrument for cutting (for adult use only)

Directions:

1. Cut large rectangles from construction paper. (These will be used as shingles for the roof.)
2. Remove one end of the box, making sure the other end is left intact.

Post Office ©1998 Monday Morning Books, Inc.

Mail Carrier House

3. Cut a pitched-roof shape on two sides of the box, as shown below.

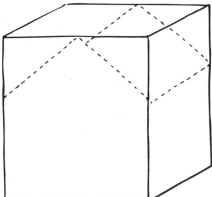

4. Cut a door and windows in the box, according to the diagram below.

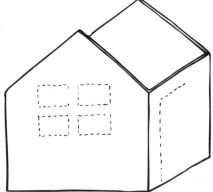

5. Cut a section out of the second appliance box for the roof, and fold it in half.

6. Trace the facial tissue box on one side of the roof and cut out. (This will become the opening for the chimney.)

Mail Carrier House

7. Punch and align holes in the roof and the pitched roof-shape box, and attach to the house and the roof with string or yarn.

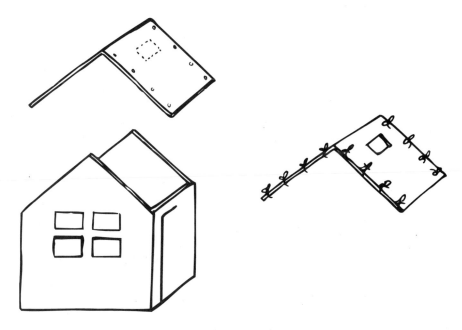

8. Insert the facial tissue box in the opening of the roof. The open end should be exposed.
9. Have children glue construction paper rectangles to the roof and chimney.
10. Have the children paint the house.
11. Place crumpled white tissue paper in the chimney for smoke.

Option:
• Old pillow cases or material can be taped to the windows for curtains.

Book Link:
• *Building a House* by Byron Barton (Greenwillow)

 Post Office ©1998 Monday Morning Books, Inc.

Flower Box

This activity should be used with the Paper Flowers (p. 27) and the Mail Carrier House (p. 23).

Materials:
Box (the size of a disposable trash bag container), Popsicle sticks, heavy string or yarn, hole punch, scissors, glue, sharp instrument for cutting (for adult use only)

Directions:
1. Remove one long side of the box.
2. Poke holes on one side of the box and under the window of the Mail Carrier House (p. 23), making sure the holes are aligned.
3. Have children glue the Popsicle sticks to three sides of the box (not the side with the holes).
4. Once the glue has dried, align the holes in the flower box with the holes under the window and secure with heavy string or yarn.

Book Link:
• *Sunflower House* by Eve Bunting (Harcourt)

Paper Flowers

Materials:
Flower and Petal Patterns (p. 28), Playdough Recipe (below), construction paper (white, red, blue, yellow, orange, and purple), markers (red, blue, yellow, orange, and purple), green pipe cleaners, scissors, glue, glue sticks

Directions:
1. Trace the flower pattern onto white construction paper and cut out. (Make one per child)
2. Use the markers to write a different color word on each section of the flowers.
3. Trace the petal pattern onto red, blue, yellow, orange, and purple construction paper. (Make one set per child.)
4. Let the children cut out the colored flower petals and match them to the color words on the flower. They can attach the petals with glue sticks.
5. Have the children punch two holes in the center of their flowers and insert pipe cleaner stems.
6. Use playdough as a base and place in the flower box.
7. Children can stick their flowers in the playdough base.

Playdough Recipe
4 cups (1 kg) flour
2 cups (.5 kg) salt
8 tsp. (40 g) cream of tartar
10 tsp. (50 ml) liquid vegetable oil
4 cups (1 l) boiling water
food coloring (desired color)

Directions:
1. Combine the first four ingredients in a large bowl.
2. Add food coloring to the boiling water.
3. Pour the water into the dry ingredients and mix.
4. Remove the dough from the bowl and knead on a floured surface.

Note:
When making this recipe with children, use extreme caution when adding boiling water.

Book Link:
• *The Tiny Seed* by Eric Carle (Picture Book Studio)

Flower and Petal Patterns

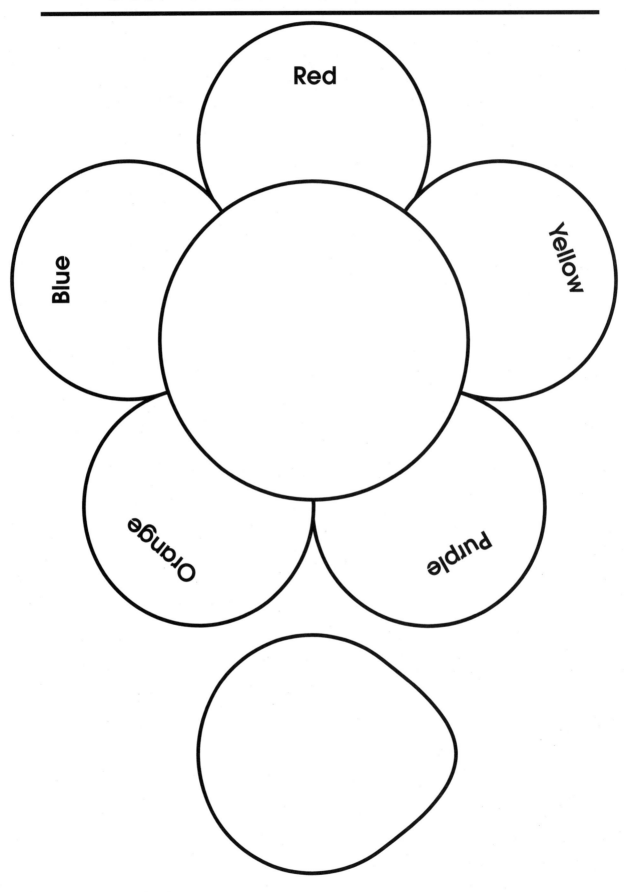

House Mailbox

Materials:

Cereal box, heavy string or yarn, tissue paper pieces (in assorted colors), white construction paper, dried beans, masking tape, marker, liquid starch, paintbrush, shallow tin (for starch), glue, scissors, sharp instrument for cutting (for adult use only)

Directions:

1. Cut a piece of white construction paper to fit the lower half of the cereal box.
2. Write large numbers on the paper.
3. Remove the inner lining from the box, and tape the lid closed.
4. Turn the box upside down and cut through three sides for a lid.
5. Poke two holes in the back of the cereal box and two holes in the front of the Mail Carrier House (p. 23). Make sure the holes are aligned.
6. Provide tissue paper pieces and liquid starch for the children to use to cover the box.
7. Let children glue dried beans on the numbers for the address.
8. Once the glue and starch have dried, glue the address to the mailbox.
9. Secure the mailbox to the house with heavy string or yarn.

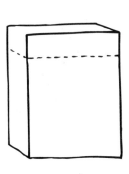

Book Link:

• *Never Mail an Elephant* by Mike Thaler (Troll)

Alphabet Toss Game

Materials:

Alphabet Patterns (pp. 31-32), 26 cardboard milk cartons (all should be the same size), construction paper, markers, stapler, bean bag

Directions:

1. Rinse out the milk cartons and cut each one in half.
2. Staple the milk cartons together to make seven rows of four cartons per row.
3. Cut construction paper into small squares, and write a letter of the alphabet on each piece of paper.
4. Place one alphabet square inside each milk carton section. (Two cartons will be empty.) Place the squares in ABC order.
5. Duplicate the Alphabet Patterns, color as desired, cut apart, laminate, and cut apart again. (Leave a thin border to prevent peeling.)
6. Teach children how to play the game. Children take turns tossing a bean bag into the alphabet box. They see where it lands and recognize the letter in the section. Then they place the alphabet pattern with a picture that begins with the same letter into that section.

Book Links:

• *The ABC Bunny* by Wanda Gag (Coward-McCann)
• *Charlie's ABC* by Mona Hatay (Hyperion)

Puzzle Link:

• *Learning the Alphabet* puzzle set (Lakeshore)

Alphabet Patterns

Alphabet Patterns

Friendship Letters

Materials:
Envelope Pattern (pp. 34-35), children's photographs (one picture of each child), white construction paper, scrap paper, crayons and markers, glue sticks, scissors, stapler, transparent tape

Directions:
1. Duplicate the envelope pattern, attach halves using transparent tape, cut out, and trace onto construction paper. (Make one per child.)
2. Help children cut out the envelopes, fold them, and staple the edges closed.
3. Have each child glue his or her photograph to the front of the envelope.
4. Write each child's name below the photograph.
5. Provide scrap paper, markers, and crayons for children to use to write letters and draw pictures for each other.
6. Hang the envelopes on a wall or bulletin board with the photographs in front.
7. Children can put their letters and pictures in their friends' envelopes.

Book Link:
• *We Are Best Friends* by Aliki (Greenwillow)

     Post Office ©1998 Monday Morning Books, Inc.

Envelope Pattern

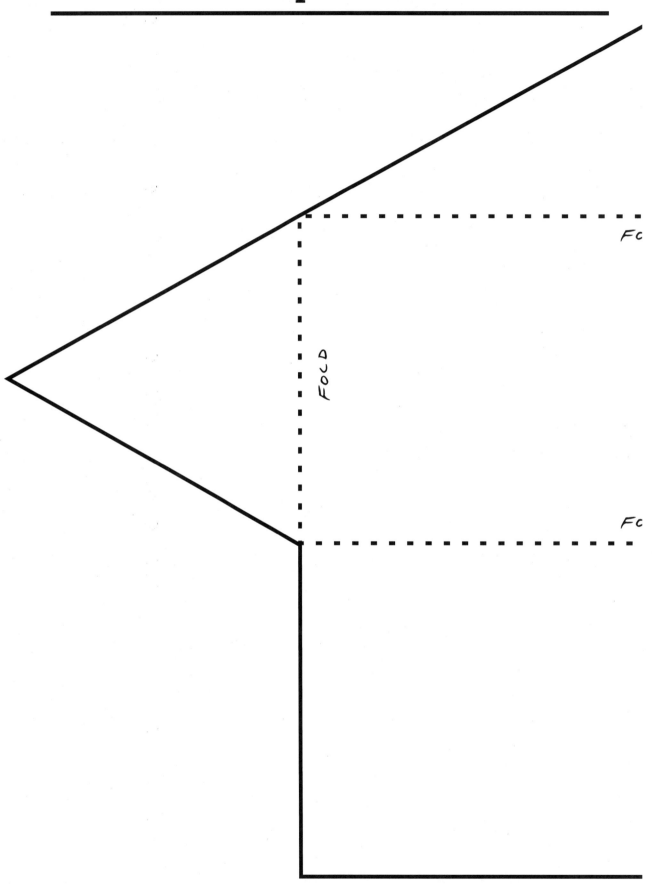

FOLD

Fc

Fc

Envelope Pattern

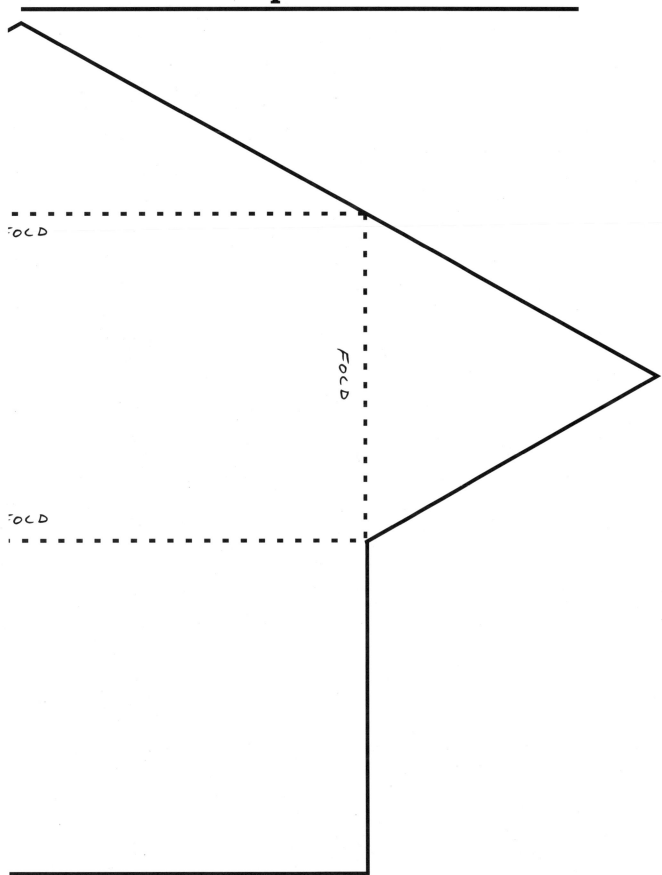

FOLD

FOLD

FOLD

Mailbox Word Game

Materials:
Animal Game Cards (p. 37), Game Board Pattern (pp. 38-39), colored markers or pens, scissors, transparent tape

Directions:
1. Duplicate the game board pattern, color, attach halves using transparent tape, and laminate.
2. Duplicate the animal game cards, cut apart, color, laminate, and cut apart again. Leave a thin border to prevent peeling.
3. Have the children match the game cards to the corresponding mailboxes on the game board.

Option:
• Use clear contact paper if a laminating machine is not available.

Book Link:
• *The A to Z Beastly Jamboree* by Robert Bender (Lodestar)

Puzzle Links:
• *Uppercase Alphabet Board* (Lakeshore)
• *Lowercase Alphabet Board* (Lakeshore)

Animal Game Cards

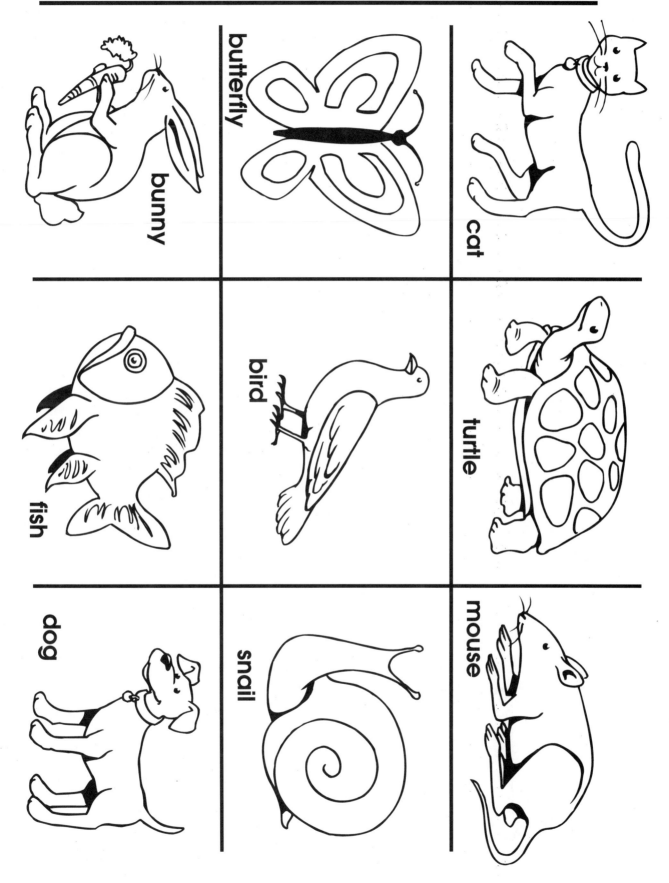

bunny

butterfly

cat

fish

bird

turtle

dog

snail

mouse

Game Board Pattern

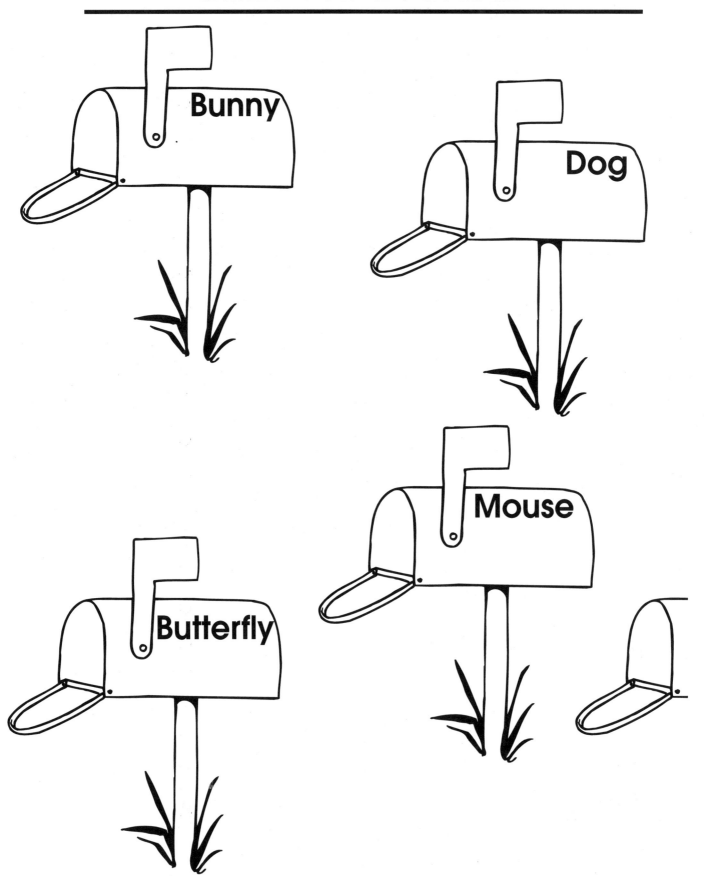

Game Board Pattern

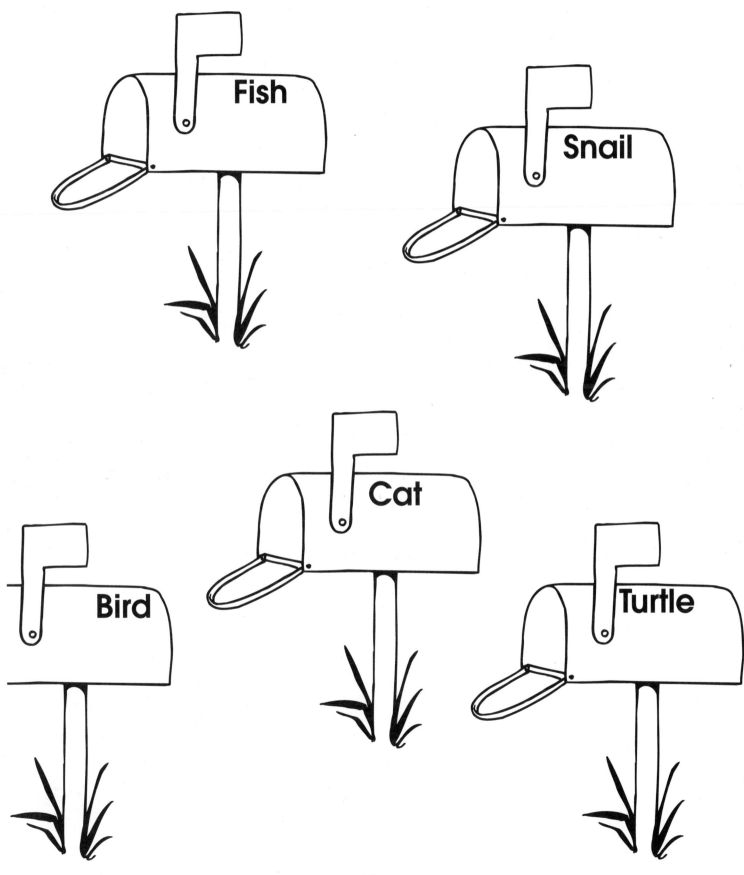

Fish

Snail

Cat

Bird

Turtle

Mail Truck Color Match

Materials:

Mail Truck Pattern (above), Mail Truck Activity Sheet (p. 41), construction paper (red, orange, yellow, green, blue, purple, black, brown, and white), markers (in same colors), scissors, glue sticks

Directions:

1. Duplicate a copy of the mail truck activity sheet for each child.
2. On each sheet, highlight the color words with markers.
3. Trace the mail truck pattern onto assorted colors of construction paper and cut out. (Make one set of trucks per child.)
4. Have children match the trucks to the activity sheet and glue them in place.

Option:

• Laminate a set of patterns and an activity sheet to be used as a matching game.

Book Link:

• *My Many Colored Days* by Dr. Seuss (Knopf)

Mail Truck Activity Sheet

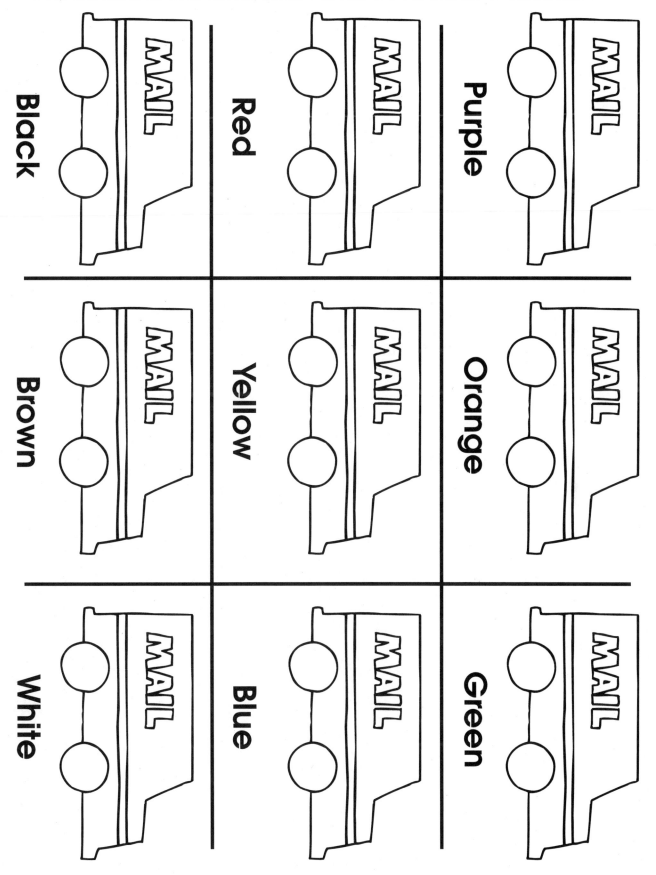

Black

Red

Purple

Brown

Yellow

Orange

White

Blue

Green

Envelope Counting

Materials:
Dot Envelopes (p. 43), Number Envelopes (p. 44), markers, scissors, envelope

Directions:
1. Duplicate a copy of each pattern, color, cut apart, laminate, and cut apart again. (Leave a thin laminate border to help prevent peeling.)
2. Spread the cards face up on a table.
3. Have children match the dot envelopes to the correct number envelopes.
4. Store the cards in an envelope when finished.

Option:
• Duplicate a copy of each pattern for each child. Let the children color the patterns and cut them apart. Have the children glue the correct dot patterns to the back of the matching number patterns. (They will have two-sided patterns, like flashcards, when they are finished.)

Puzzle Link:
• *Number Puzzle Board* (Lakeshore)

Dot Envelopes

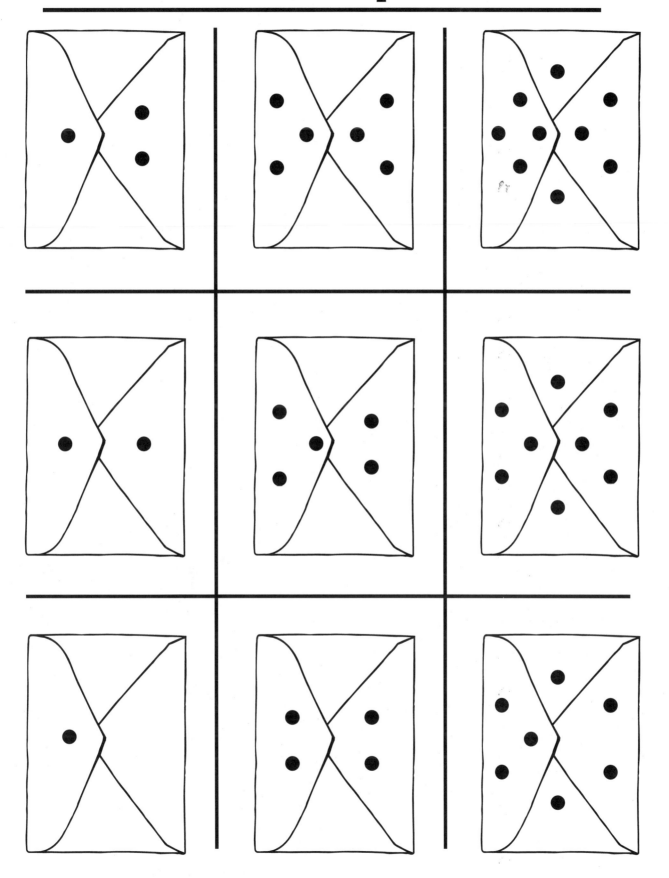

Post Office ©1998 Monday Morning Books, Inc.

Number Envelopes

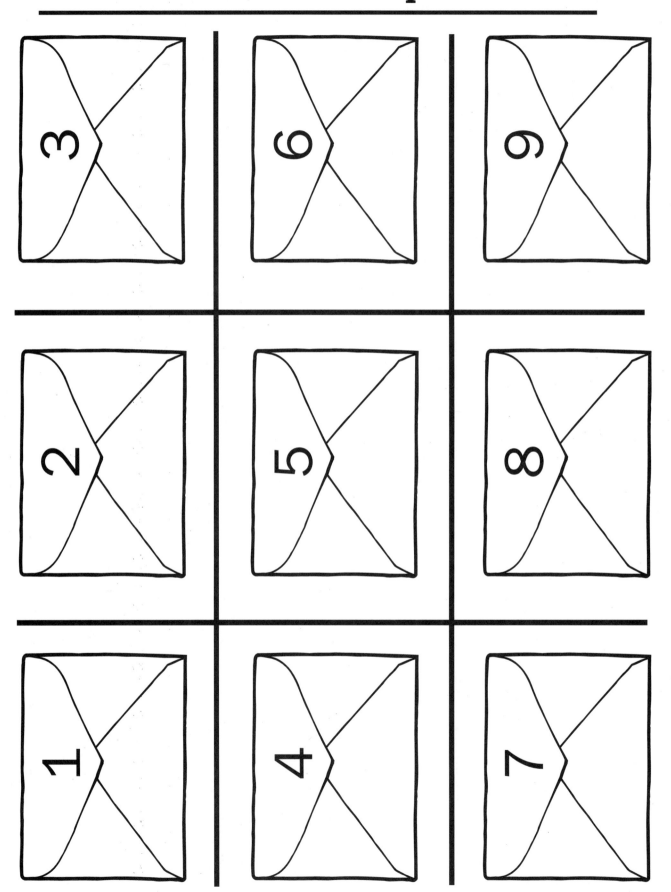

Post Office Puzzle

Materials:
Post Office Puzzle (p. 46), plain paper, scissors, glue or glue sticks, crayons or markers, envelopes (optional)

Directions:
1. Duplicate one copy of the post office puzzle for each child.
2. Let the children color their puzzles and cut them apart on the dotted lines.
3. Children can either glue the puzzle pieces onto plain paper backgrounds, or they can store the puzzle pieces in envelopes to play with on other days.

   Post Office ©1998 Monday Morning Books, Inc.

Post Office Puzzle

Post Office Memory Match

Materials:
Post Office Patterns (p. 48), colored markers, scissors, clear contact paper

Directions:
1. Duplicate the post office patterns twice, color, cut apart, cover with contact paper or laminate, and cut out again. (Leave a thin laminate border around each pattern to help prevent peeling.)
2. Shuffle the cards and spread them face down on a table.
3. Demonstrate how to play the game. The object is to match the post office patterns by turning the cards over two at a time. If a match is made, the cards remain face up and the child takes another turn. If a match is not made, the cards are turned over and the next child takes a turn. The game continues until all cards are face up.

Option:
• Introduce the game by leaving the shuffled cards face up and having the children simply match the post office patterns together.

Post Office Patterns